The Israeli-Palestinian Conflict

A Comprehensive History from World War II to the Present Day

The Israeli-Palestinian Conflict A Comprehensive History from World War II to the Present Day

Tony Apindi

Published by Tony Apindi, 2023.

THE ISRAELI-PALESTINIAN CONFLICT A COMPREHENSIVE HISTORY FROM WORLD WAR II TO THE PRESENT DAY

First edition. October 14, 2023.

Copyright © 2023 Tony Apindi.

ISBN: 979-8223781110

Written by Tony Apindi.

Table of Contents

To all the individuals, on both sides of the Israeli-Palestinian conflict, who have tirelessly pursued the dream of peace. Your unwavering hope, resilience, and commitment to a brighter future inspire us all. This book is dedicated to you, as a testament to the possibility of reconciliation, understanding, and coexistence. May your efforts pave the way for a more peaceful world.

Chapter 1

The Roots of the Conflict

The Israeli-Palestinian conflict, a saga spanning over a century, is a complex and enduring enigma with no quick fixes or simple solutions. At its core, this intricate conflict finds its origins in the late 19th century, when the nascent Zionist movement took its first steps towards shaping the course of history. Zionism, a profound movement with a vision of establishing a Jewish homeland in the Land of Israel, laid the groundwork for a contentious struggle that would unfold over the decades.

The Land of Israel, the epicenter of this conflict, holds profound significance for both Jews and Muslims. For Jews, it is the Promised Land, a testament to their ancient heritage, and an embodiment of their religious devotion. Muslims, too, hold this land dear, considering it the third holiest site in Islam, with historical and religious roots that are deeply intertwined with the region. During this era, the Land of Israel found itself under the rule of the Ottoman Empire, a sprawling empire that spanned across North Africa and the Middle East. The Ottoman Empire was predominantly Muslim, mirroring the demographic composition of the Land of Israel. However, in the late 19th and early 20th centuries, the seeds of conflict were sown as a growing number of Jews sought refuge in the Land of Israel. This wave of Jewish immigration was propelled by a confluence of factors, including persecution in Europe and a yearning to return to their ancestral homeland.

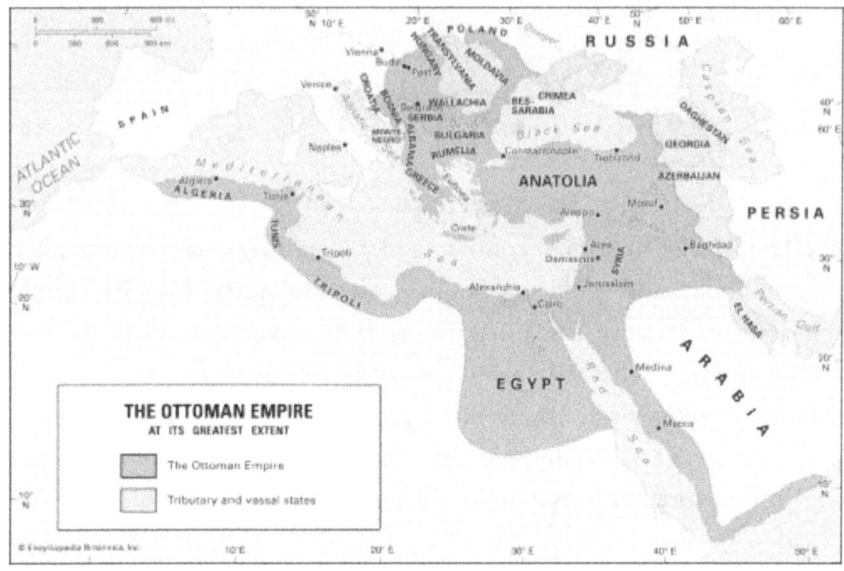

Map of the Ottoman Empire (Photo courtesy of Encyclopedia Britannica Inc.)

AS JEWISH IMMIGRANTS settled in the region, the Zionist movement embarked on a mission to purchase land and establish Jewish settlements. This endeavor ignited tension with the Arab population, who harbored fears that these new arrivals were intent on seizing control of the Land of Israel. Following World War I, the Ottoman Empire crumbled, and the Land of Palestine came under the mandate of the British Empire. This mandate entrusted the British with the responsibility of governing the territory until it could attain independence. However, during this period, the Jewish population in the Land of Israel continued to grow, and the British facilitated more Jewish immigration. This demographic shift further stoked the flames of discord as the Arab population felt that the British were favoring the Zionist cause. The culmination of these tensions came to a head in 1936 when the Arab population launched a full-scale revolt against British rule, an uprising that persisted for three years before being quashed by British forces.

The post-World War II era was marked by a pivotal event that reshaped the course of history: the Holocaust. During this dark period in Europe, the Nazis perpetrated the genocide of six million Jews. The Holocaust galvanized the international community to recognize the need for a Jewish homeland. In 1947, the United Nations passed a resolution to partition the Land of Palestine into two states, one Jewish and one Arab. While the Jewish population in the region accepted this plan, the Arab population vehemently rejected it. In the tumultuous year of 1948, the State of Israel was declared, setting the stage for the 1948 Arab-Israeli War. This conflict endured for eight months, concluding with an Israeli victory. Yet, the cost of this victory was immense. Hundreds of thousands of Palestinians were forcibly displaced from their homes, their lives forever altered. These displaced Palestinians became refugees, and their legacy endures in the refugee camps that still dot the landscape of the region today. The 1948 War served as a stark turning point, marking the inception of a protracted conflict that has raged for over 70 years. The Israeli-Palestinian conflict is an intricate web of historical events, political decisions, and human experiences, and as we delve deeper into its layers, it becomes evident that there are no easy answers.

In the chapters to follow, we will unravel the intricate tapestry of this complex struggle, exploring the major events and pivotal moments that have shaped its course. This conflict is a puzzle, and as we piece it together, we will gain a deeper understanding of the challenges and aspirations of both sides, the myriad perspectives, and the complexities that lie ahead. In Chapter 2, *"The 1948 War and the Establishment of the State of Israel,"* we will journey through the tumultuous period surrounding the birth of the State of Israel and the consequences that reverberated across the region. We'll delve into the major battles and the human stories that unfolded during this defining chapter in the conflict's history.

Chapter 2

The 1948 War and the Establishment of the State of Israel

The year 1948 bore witness to a profound transformation in the Middle East - the birth of the State of Israel, and the eruption of the first Arab-Israeli War. This conflict, which lasted for eight tumultuous months, culminated in an Israeli victory. As the pages of history unfurl, we delve into the pivotal moments of this war, and the profound implications it had for both Israelis and Palestinians.

David Ben Gurion reading the Declaration of Independence of the State of Israel
(Courtesy of Ministry of Foreign Affairs of Israel)

THE WAR'S COMMENCEMENT on May 15, 1948, was a mere day after Israel declared its independence. Five Arab nations - Egypt, Syria, Iraq, Lebanon, and Transjordan - swiftly invaded Israel, driven by a mix of political, ideological, and strategic motives. On paper, the Arab forces held numerical and equipment advantages over the fledgling Israeli military. However, the Israeli army, comprised of individuals with an unwavering commitment and well-honed organization, was poised to defy the odds. The initial phases of the war saw a series of successes for the Arab armies. However, in the summer of 1948, the Israelis managed to turn the tide. By year's end, the Arab armies were defeated, and Israel had extended its territorial boundaries far beyond the confines originally set by the United Nations' partition plan. The cost of this victory was steep. Hundreds of thousands of Palestinians found themselves forcibly displaced from their homes, leaving behind the familiar landscapes of their lives. These dispossessed Palestinians became refugees, a legacy that continues to endure in the refugee camps that punctuate the region's landscape today.

The 1948 War not only marked the beginning of the Israeli-Palestinian conflict but also cast a long shadow that continues to influence the course of history. The conflict has raged for over seven decades, and its resolution remains elusive. As we journey forward in this book, we will unravel the complexities, motivations, and consequences that emanated from this pivotal moment, providing a more comprehensive understanding of the ongoing struggle.

The Aftermath of the War

The aftermath of the 1948 War ushered in a period of profound upheaval and uncertainty, with far-reaching implications for the Middle East and beyond. This pivotal conflict, also known as the War of Independence, concluded with a series of consequences that continue to reverberate in the region to this day. Notably, the war resulted in the displacement of hundreds of thousands of Palestinians from their ancestral homes, many of whom found themselves in refugee camps in neighboring countries. These camps, located in Jordan, Lebanon, Syria, and the Gaza Strip, became enduring symbols of the conflict's human cost. They are a stark reminder of the lasting impact of the 1948 War and the unresolved issue of Palestinian displacement.

Moreover, the war led to the establishment of a new boundary, known as the Green Line, which physically separated Israel from its Arab neighbors. However, this demarcation remains unrecognized on the international stage, with both Israel and the Palestinians asserting claims to territories beyond its borders. The Green Line delineates the border established by the 1949 Armistice Agreements, but the conflict's enduring legacy of territorial disputes has kept these boundaries in a state of flux. The Green Line represents both a geographical and symbolic dividing line between Israelis and Palestinians, serving as a poignant reminder of the unresolved territorial issues that continue to hamper the peace process. Furthermore, the 1948 War's bitter legacy left a deep and lasting wellspring of mistrust between Israelis and Palestinians. This lingering discord has given rise to numerous confrontations and clashes over the years, perpetuating the cycle of violence and impeding the pursuit of a peaceful resolution. The mutual distrust has often resulted in setbacks during peace negotiations and created hurdles in building a foundation of trust necessary for any lasting resolution to the Israeli-Palestinian conflict. Thus, the consequences of the 1948 War, with its displacement, boundary disputes, and the persistence of mutual mistrust, continue to shape the dynamics of the conflict, further emphasizing the need for comprehensive peace efforts.

The Palestinian Refugee Crisis

The Palestinian Refugee Crisis, arguably one of the most enduring and poignant consequences of the 1948 War, is deeply intertwined with the conflict's historical and human dimensions. This crisis stems from the displacement of hundreds of thousands of Palestinians who were dispossessed during the war and its aftermath. Many of these displaced individuals and their descendants still reside in refugee camps, primarily located in Jordan, Lebanon, Syria, and the Gaza Strip. These camps are poignant symbols of the ongoing humanitarian tragedy, where the living conditions are often harsh, marked by overcrowding and limited access to education, employment, and essential services. The Palestinian refugee crisis holds profound implications for the pursuit of peace in the Middle East. At its core is the issue of the right of return, where the displaced Palestinians, along with their descendants, assert their right to return to their ancestral homes. This right has been consistently denied by Israel, and it stands as one of the most contentious and unresolved issues in the conflict. Additionally, the refugees seek compensation for their losses, a request that has yet to be met by Israel. The Palestinian refugee crisis embodies the enduring pain and suffering caused by the 1948 War, and it continues to be a central obstacle to comprehensive peace efforts.

Two women and one child in front of their house of sorts in the heart of Gaza. Apart from their appalling living conditions, Gazan parents find themselves unable to meet their children's basic needs such as food, health and housing. (Courtesy of WFP/Wissam Nassar)

THE ISRAELI-PALESTINIAN Conflict Today

As we fast forward to the present, the Israeli-Palestinian conflict remains far from resolution. The two sides have yet to find common ground, and the cycle of violence endures. This conflict is a multidimensional one, with numerous perspectives on the issue. For some, it's a clash of religious significance, while others view it through the lens of land and sovereignty. Resolution pathways remain contentious as well. Some advocate for a two-state solution, with Israel and Palestine coexisting in peace. Others propose a one-state solution, envisioning a single, shared state for both Israelis and Palestinians. The Israeli-Palestinian conflict, a daunting challenge, is not inherently intractable. Hope for peace remains, but it requires courage and compromise from all parties involved.

As we delve deeper into the chapters that follow, we shall continue to explore the multifaceted dimensions of this complex conflict. By understanding its origins, consequences, and the profound human experiences within, we take a step closer to comprehending the intricate tapestry of the Israeli-Palestinian saga.

Chapter 3

The Six-Day War and the Israeli Occupation

The year 1967 ushered in a pivotal moment in the history of the Israeli-Palestinian conflict, with the eruption of the Six-Day War in June. This six-day conflict culminated in a resounding victory for Israel, reshaping the landscape of the Middle East and setting the stage for enduring tension.

Courtesy (The New Arab)

A PRELUDE TO CONFLICT

The Six-Day War in June 1967 was not an isolated event; it was the culmination of years of mounting tensions and regional dynamics that set the stage for the conflict. The lead-up to the war was marked by a series of factors and actions that heightened the risk of a military confrontation in the Middle East. One of the primary drivers of the mounting tension was the ongoing Arab-Israeli conflict. Since the establishment of the State of Israel in 1948, Arab states, particularly Egypt and Jordan, had been in a state of conflict with Israel. Border clashes, skirmishes, and acts of violence had been recurring features during this period. Additionally, the situation in the Gaza Strip and the West Bank, which were under Egyptian and Jordanian control respectively, contributed to the rising tensions. These territories had been used as bases for Palestinian guerrilla attacks into Israel, intensifying the security concerns of the Israeli government. Moreover, there were political and military developments on the Arab side that further raised concerns in Israel. Egypt's President Gamal Abdel Nasser's aggressive rhetoric, his military buildup in the Sinai Peninsula, and his decision to expel the United Nations Emergency Force (UNEF) from the Sinai in May 1967 all alarmed Israel. Nasser's actions were perceived as a direct threat to Israel's security and led to a sense of imminent danger.

Against this backdrop of mounting tension and perceived threats, Israel's decision to launch a preemptive strike on June 5, 1967, was driven by the need to neutralize what it perceived as an impending attack by Egypt. The success of Israel's initial strike was swift and marked by the rapid defeat of the Egyptian military. Israel also engaged and emerged victorious against the Syrian and Jordanian armies during the war. The Six-Day War, with its rapid and decisive outcomes, had profound and far-reaching consequences for the region, including the Israeli occupation of the Gaza Strip, West Bank, and East Jerusalem. It was a conflict that not only reshaped the political and territorial landscape but also intensified the Israeli-Palestinian conflict, with repercussions felt to this day.

Consequences of Victory

The consequences of the Six-Day War were profound and multifaceted. Israel's capture of the Sinai Peninsula, Gaza Strip, West Bank, and Golan Heights dramatically reshaped the geopolitical landscape of the Middle East. These territories, now under Israeli occupation, became central points of contention and remain at the heart of the Israeli-Palestinian conflict.

The war's outcome had a significant impact on Israel. While celebrated by its citizens for achieving victory, it also presented formidable challenges. The capture of new territories meant an increased responsibility for governing and administering these regions, including their Palestinian populations. This led to significant demographic, security, and economic complexities for Israel, contributing to the ongoing complexities of the conflict. In contrast, neighboring Arab countries viewed Israel's victory with consternation. The loss of territory was a significant blow to their prestige and military capabilities. Additionally, the Palestinian territories became a focal point of Arab nationalism, with Arab states expressing solidarity with the Palestinian cause.

The international community closely monitored the aftermath of the war. The United Nations passed Resolution 242, calling for the withdrawal of Israeli armed forces from the territories occupied during the conflict and recognition of the right to live in peace and security for all states in the region. However, this resolution's implementation and subsequent peace negotiations proved challenging, perpetuating the Israeli-Palestinian conflict for decades to come.

The Israeli Occupation

The Israeli occupation of the Palestinian territories has been a source of continuous tension and violence. Since the 1948 War, Palestinians have been steadfast in their quest for independence, but the occupation has posed immense challenges to their aspirations. The occupation has taken a heavy toll on the Palestinian population, with reports of human rights abuses including arbitrary arrests and detentions, instances of torture, and the destruction of homes. These conditions have created an atmosphere of perpetual uncertainty and vulnerability for the Palestinian people. The economic implications of the occupation have also reverberated. Israel has invested substantial resources in maintaining the occupation, diverting billions of dollars that could have been allocated to education, healthcare, and infrastructure development. The economic disparities between Israelis and Palestinians in the occupied territories have widened, deepening the sense of injustice and resentment.

The Peace Process and its Failures

In the aftermath of the Six-Day War, a multitude of attempts were made to find a peaceful resolution to the Israeli-Palestinian conflict. These initiatives, however, were fraught with challenges that ultimately led to a series of failed peace initiatives. Among the most significant of these efforts was the Oslo Accords, signed in 1993. The Oslo Accords represented a comprehensive framework aimed at laying the groundwork for a two-state solution, envisioning Israel and Palestine coexisting in peace. Sadly, the full implementation of the Oslo Accords remained elusive, and the peace process began to unravel in 2000.

Subsequent years witnessed various attempts to reignite the peace process, but none managed to achieve the desired results. The conflict remained deeply entrenched, with both sides clinging to long-standing grievances and entrenched distrust. The Oslo Accords marked a pivotal moment in the pursuit of peace, as they introduced the concept of Palestinian self-governance in parts of the West Bank and Gaza Strip. They established the Palestinian Authority and aimed to facilitate a gradual transfer of power to Palestinians. However, issues such as borders, refugees, security, and the status of Jerusalem remained highly contentious, causing peace negotiations to falter. The Second Intifada, a violent Palestinian uprising that began in 2000, dealt a significant blow to the peace process. This conflict, characterized by suicide bombings, shootings, and reprisals by the Israeli military, resulted in a sharp escalation of violence and a breakdown in trust between the two sides. Peace negotiations became increasingly difficult in such a hostile environment.

In the years that followed, the peace process encountered numerous roadblocks, from disputes over settlements to disagreements over the sequencing of negotiations. International efforts to mediate between the parties, including the United States' involvement, have yielded limited success. The unresolved status of Jerusalem and the right of return for Palestinian refugees have remained formidable obstacles to achieving a comprehensive peace agreement.

The Future and the Path to Peace

The future of the Israeli-Palestinian conflict is fraught with uncertainty. Key issues remain divisive, and a peaceful resolution appears distant. Nonetheless, it is vital to remember that peace remains an attainable goal. The annals of history are replete with conflicts that have been resolved peacefully, and the Israeli-Palestinian conflict can be no exception. Ultimately, the path to peace rests in the hands of Israel and Palestine's leaders. Should they choose the path of peace, it will necessitate compromise and a commitment to coexistence. A future where both nations share the land in harmony is conceivable, but it requires the courage and vision to break free from the cycle of violence and mistrust.

As we traverse the following chapters, we will continue to unearth the intricate tapestry of this enduring conflict. With each page turned, we come closer to comprehending the complexities, challenges, and, above all, the possibilities for peace in the Israeli-Palestinian saga.

Chapter 4

The Yom Kippur War

In October 1973, the world bore witness to the Yom Kippur War, a conflict that unfolded between Israel and its Arab neighbors. This war was initiated on Yom Kippur, the holiest day in the Jewish calendar, and it was launched as a surprise attack by Egypt and Syria, with the aim of reclaiming territory lost in the Six-Day War.

The War That Shook the World

The Yom Kippur War, also known as the October War or the Ramadan War in the Arab world, shook the world with its audacious timing and ferocity. As the haunting sound of the shofar marked the beginning of Yom Kippur, Jewish communities around the world were preparing for a day of fasting and prayer. Little did they know that a storm was brewing in the Middle East, one that would have profound global implications. The war was not just a military conflict; it was a collision of cultures, ideologies, and historical narratives.

The timing of the Yom Kippur War was striking. It began on October 6, 1973, which coincided with the holiest day in the Jewish calendar, Yom Kippur. This deliberate timing added a layer of symbolism and significance to the conflict. The audacity of launching an attack on this sacred day underscored the deeply rooted enmity between the Arab states, primarily Egypt and Syria, and Israel. The Yom Kippur War was not confined to the battlefield; it extended its impact to the global stage. It drew the attention of superpowers like the United States and the Soviet Union, who were drawn into the conflict by their alliances with the warring parties. The war became a proxy battleground for the Cold War rivals. The consequences of this conflict reverberated far beyond the region, shaping geopolitics and diplomacy for years to come.

The Battle Begins

On the fateful day of October 6, 1973, the Middle East plunged into turmoil as Egypt and Syria executed a meticulously coordinated assault against Israel. This attack was executed with precision and audacity, catching Israel off guard on a day of profound significance to the Jewish faith. Egypt's military crossed the Suez Canal and made deep advances into the Sinai Peninsula, while the Syrian armed forces launched a simultaneous assault on the Golan Heights. The world watched in shock and awe as the Arab armies, equipped with modern Soviet weaponry and advanced tactics, confronted the Israeli Defense Forces, a force well-known for its military prowess.

The initial stages of the Yom Kippur War found Israel facing formidable challenges. The shock of the surprise attack was compounded by the sophistication of the weaponry and tactics employed by the Arab forces. Israeli soldiers and civilians experienced harrowing moments as they grappled with the sudden onslaught. The Arab forces made significant territorial gains, capturing strategic positions in the Sinai Peninsula and the Golan Heights, territories occupied by Israel since the Six-Day War in 1967. Despite the initial setbacks, Israel's response to the Yom Kippur War was characterized by rapid mobilization, resilience, and determined counteroffensives. The nation underwent a massive effort to regroup, call up reserves, and push back against the Arab advances. The Israeli Air Force played a pivotal role in achieving air superiority, while ground forces initiated a series of fierce counterattacks.

One of the most remarkable turnarounds of the Yom Kippur War was Israel's resilience and ability to regain the initiative. The ferocity of the conflict, with both sides sustaining heavy casualties, led to intense battles across the frontlines. In the Sinai Peninsula, Israel launched Operation Gazelle, employing a combination of tank and infantry tactics to push the Egyptian forces back. On the Golan Heights, Israeli forces faced determined Syrian resistance but managed to recapture territory.

The Cost of Victory

By the war's conclusion, Israel had successfully pushed back the Arab armies to their pre-war positions. However, the victory came at a high price, with over 2,500 Israeli casualties. The war's impact rippled into the Israeli economy, leading to a period of economic hardship and uncertainty. The Yom Kippur War was not just a military victory; it was a humbling experience for Israel. It shattered the illusion of invincibility and made the world realize that even a nation born in the fires of conflict could face existential threats. It was a stark reminder that the Middle East was a region where the winds of war could change direction at any moment.

The War That Changed the Game

The Yom Kippur War, which unfolded in October 1973, marked a critical inflection point in the Israeli-Palestinian conflict and the broader geopolitical dynamics of the region. For Israel, this conflict brought a startling revelation: the nation was not immune to military threats. The surprise attack by the combined forces of Egypt and Syria on Yom Kippur, the holiest day in Judaism, caught Israel off guard and exposed the vulnerabilities in its defense posture. The initial setbacks and heavy casualties endured by the Israeli Defense Forces during the war served as a stark reminder of the human cost of conflict. It prompted a profound reevaluation of Israeli policies and strategies, initiating a transformative process that would ultimately influence their approach to peace negotiations.

Perhaps the most intriguing consequence of the Yom Kippur War was the apparent shift in Israeli willingness to engage in negotiations for a peaceful resolution with the Palestinians. The conflict was a moment of deep introspection for Israel, fostering a growing recognition of the imperative to find a way to coexist with their neighbors. The trauma of war led many Israelis to question the sustainability of an indefinite state of conflict. It made them reflect on the sacrifices made and the profound losses endured by both sides, sparking a desire to explore alternatives to protracted hostilities. This moment of reflection laid the groundwork for a shift in Israeli public opinion and, ultimately, a more conciliatory approach toward the possibility of peace negotiations. In the years following the Yom Kippur War, Israel began to engage in a series of diplomatic efforts aimed at finding a peaceful resolution to the Israeli-Palestinian conflict. While significant challenges and obstacles remained, the war's legacy continued to influence the nation's approach to negotiations. The Yom Kippur War had, in many ways, opened a door to a new era of reflection, debate, and a growing realization among Israelis that a peaceful resolution with the Palestinians was not only desirable but also necessary for their own security and well-being. The war had changed the game, pushing Israel toward a more proactive role in the pursuit of peace and contributing to the evolving narrative of the Israeli-Palestinian conflict.

The Aftermath and Political Shifts

The aftermath of the Yom Kippur War carried significant political reverberations, reshaping the landscape of both Israel and the broader Arab world. Internally, Israel experienced a momentous political shift, notably during the 1977 general election. The long-standing dominance of the Labor Party, which had held power since Israel's establishment, came to an end. The victory of the Likud Party, led by Menachem Begin, marked a significant turning point in Israel's political trajectory. The Likud Party adopted a more hawkish stance, emphasizing a security-first approach and exhibiting a diminished willingness to engage in compromises with the Palestinians.

The ascendancy of Likud to power and the ideological differences between the parties had profound implications for the Israeli-Palestinian conflict. It signaled a more conservative and uncompromising approach, at least in the short term, which would shape Israel's policies and strategies in the following years. The impact of this political transformation was palpable in subsequent negotiations and peace initiatives. The Yom Kippur War not only reshaped Israeli politics but also had a pronounced effect on the Arab world. While the conflict initially appeared to be a united front against Israel, the war unveiled the inherent divisions and disunity among Arab states. The response to the conflict underscored the limits of Arab solidarity in supporting the Palestinian cause. The war exposed the internal divisions, rivalries, and competing interests among Arab states, as well as the priority each nation assigned to its own concerns over the Palestinian issue. This revealed the intricacies and challenges of maintaining a unified Arab stance, ultimately leading to a waning of support for the Palestinians on the regional stage.

The Yom Kippur War, therefore, had far-reaching political consequences that extended beyond the battlefield. It shifted the dynamics of the Israeli-Palestinian conflict and reshaped the political landscape within Israel. Simultaneously, it laid bare the complexities of maintaining a united Arab front and raised questions about the extent of support for the Palestinian cause in the wider Arab world. These post-war political shifts would have enduring implications for the course of the Israeli-Palestinian conflict and the pursuit of peace in the region.

A Glimmer of Hope: The Peace Process

The aftermath of the Yom Kippur War introduced a renewed and compelling interest in finding a resolution to the Israeli-Palestinian conflict. In 1978, a significant development occurred when Israel and Egypt reached the Camp David Accords, a bilateral agreement facilitated by the United States. This landmark agreement led to Israel's withdrawal from the Sinai Peninsula, marking the first time an Arab nation formally recognized the State of Israel. While the Camp David Accords constituted a historic breakthrough in regional relations, they did not encompass a comprehensive solution to the Israeli-Palestinian conflict, focusing primarily on the Egyptian-Israeli relationship.

One noteworthy aspect of the Camp David Accords was the absence of Palestinian representation at the negotiations. The Palestinian leadership and people viewed themselves as marginalized and left out of the process, deepening their sense of abandonment. As a result, the

Palestinians boycotted the Camp David peace negotiations, adamant that their aspirations for self-determination and statehood had not been addressed. The years following the Camp David Accords witnessed numerous international efforts to broker a peace agreement between Israel and the Palestinians. These attempts aimed to tackle the core issues of the conflict, including the delineation of borders, the status of Jerusalem, and the fate of Palestinian refugees. However, these endeavors encountered significant challenges, primarily the enduring gaps between the two parties on these fundamental matters. Despite these attempts, the Israeli-Palestinian conflict remained unresolved, casting a long shadow over the region. The Camp David Accords may have signaled a glimmer of hope, but the path to a comprehensive peace agreement between Israelis and Palestinians remained a complex and elusive one, with significant hurdles yet to be overcome.

Israeli Prime Minister Menahem begin with Egyptian President Anwar Sadat and resident Jimmy Carter during their peace talks on September 6, 1978 at the Presidential retreat at Camp David in Maryland. (Courtesy: Jesse Greenspan history.com)

THE ELUSIVE PEACE

The future of the Israeli-Palestinian conflict remains shrouded in uncertainty. Core issues continue to divide the two sides, and the path to peace remains elusive. Yet, it is imperative to hold onto the hope that peace can be attained. History is replete with examples of conflicts that found peaceful resolutions, and the Israeli-Palestinian conflict is no exception. The responsibility for peace lies in the hands of Israeli and Palestinian leaders. Should they choose this path, it will demand compromises and a shared vision of coexistence. While the challenges persist, so too does the potential for a future in which both nations inhabit the same land in harmony.

As we proceed through the following chapters, we continue to unveil the multifaceted dimensions of this enduring conflict. Each page brings us closer to comprehending the complexities, challenges, and the vision of peace within the Israeli-Palestinian narrative. In the chapters ahead, we will explore the numerous attempts, negotiations, and the aspirations of people on both sides of this deeply rooted conflict, as they strive to find a path to peace in a troubled land.

Chapter 5

The First Intifada

The late 1980s and early 1990s witnessed a seismic shift in the Israeli-Palestinian conflict with the emergence of the First Intifada, also known as the Great Uprising. This sustained series of civil disobedience measures, protests, and violent riots took place in the Israeli-occupied West Bank and Gaza Strip, signifying a turning point in the struggle for Palestinian rights.

Palestinians demonstrate in Nablus on the West Bank on Jan. 22, 1988. While mass protests grabbed headlines, the Intifada was powered by a grassroots democratic network of co-ops, women's groups, community councils and more. (Sven Nackstrand/AFP/Getty Images)

THE SPARK OF THE INTIFADA

The spark for the Intifada ignited on December 9, 1987, when an Israeli Defense Forces (IDF) truck collided with a civilian car, leading to the tragic deaths of four Palestinian workers, three of whom hailed from the Jabalya refugee camp. Palestinians alleged that the collision was a deliberate act of retaliation for the earlier killing of an Israeli in Gaza. Israel, on the other hand, denied any intent or coordination in the crash, despite the heightened tensions at the time. In response, Palestinians across the territories engaged in protests, civil disobedience, and, at times, violent acts.

UNDERLYING FACTORS

The First Intifada, also known as the Great Uprising, was a multifaceted and deeply rooted movement that found its impetus in a confluence of factors, reflecting the complex tapestry of the Israeli-Palestinian conflict:

- *Prolonged Occupation*

One of the central sparks of the First Intifada was the prolonged Israeli occupation of the West Bank and Gaza Strip. This occupation had extended into its 20th year, engendering a profound sense of frustration and despair among Palestinians. The absence of political self-determination, coupled with the daily hardships imposed by occupation, had created a volatile climate of discontent. The desire for autonomy and freedom from occupation became a powerful motivating force.

- *Israeli Settlement Policy*

Israel's ongoing settlement policy in the occupied territories served as another major source of tension. This policy entailed the construction of Jewish settlements on land claimed by Palestinians, resulting in the gradual expansion of Israeli control over the West Bank and Gaza. The growth of these settlements not only altered the physical and demographic landscape but also presented a significant impediment to the establishment of a future Palestinian state. The encroachment of settlements became a visible symbol of Israeli dominance, further fueling Palestinian grievances.

- *Economic Hardships*

Economic hardships were pervasive in the Palestinian territories and significantly contributed to the unrest that led to the First Intifada. High unemployment rates, limited access to essential resources, and inadequate infrastructure development had created an environment of hardship and suffering. The economic difficulties, particularly high levels of unemployment, affected the daily lives of Palestinians, amplifying their sense of frustration and despair.

- *Lack of Progress in Peace Talks*

The failure of peace negotiations to make substantial progress was a deeply disillusioning factor. Despite various attempts to negotiate a peaceful resolution to the conflict, core issues such as borders, the rights of Palestinian refugees, and the status of Jerusalem remained unaddressed. The lack of headway in resolving these critical issues left Palestinians disheartened and skeptical about the prospects for peace. It underscored the need for a more active and assertive approach to achieve their aspirations.

These underlying factors, entwined with a shared aspiration for self-determination and independence, fueled the First Intifada. The collective discontent, combined with a desire for change, transformed into a sustained series of civil disobedience measures, protests, and at times, violent confrontations, marking a significant turning point in the struggle for Palestinian rights and the broader Israeli-Palestinian conflict.

Duration and Impact

The First Intifada, spanning six years, from 1987 to 1993, was a significant chapter in the Israeli-Palestinian conflict. This protracted period of unrest resulted in substantial human and economic costs on both sides. Over 1,000 Palestinians and more than 150 Israelis lost their lives during this tumultuous period. Beyond the tragic loss of life, the First Intifada had far-reaching social, political, and economic consequences. The Intifada was characterized by a form of resistance that involved Palestinian youths using stones and Molotov cocktails against heavily armed Israeli forces. These young protesters, armed with rudimentary weapons, became symbolic figures of the resistance. It was a time marked by daily confrontations, street clashes, curfews, and violence in the streets of the occupied territories.

The sustained uprising captured the attention of the international community, resulting in a surge of global awareness and sympathy for the Palestinian cause. The images of Palestinian youths facing Israeli soldiers were broadcast on television screens worldwide, evoking powerful emotions and increasing the understanding of the Palestinians' plight. The world watched as Palestinians sought to assert their right to self-determination and freedom. The international spotlight on the First Intifada exerted pressure on Israel to address the root causes of the conflict and engage in a more substantive and meaningful peace process. The images of Palestinian suffering and their struggle for independence sparked calls for a resolution to the long-standing Israeli-Palestinian conflict.

The Intifada's End and the Oslo Accords

The end of the First Intifada in 1993 marked a significant turning point in the Israeli-Palestinian conflict with the signing of the Oslo Accords. These accords, a series of agreements between Israel and the Palestinian Liberation Organization (PLO), were brokered with the assistance of the United States, Russia, and facilitated by Norway. The Oslo Accords aimed to lay the groundwork for a two-state solution, which would end the decades-long conflict. The agreements garnered international attention and were celebrated as a significant breakthrough in the peace process. One of the key aspects of the Oslo Accords was the establishment of the Palestinian Authority, which would govern parts of the West Bank and Gaza Strip. This move was seen as a step toward Palestinian self-governance, granting them a degree of control over their affairs.

Despite this progress, the ultimate goal of a two-state solution and the resolution of core issues like borders, the status of Jerusalem, and the right of return for Palestinian refugees remained a challenge. The Oslo Accords created a framework for negotiations, but the thorniest issues were left for future discussions.

Impact and Legacy

The First Intifada left a profound impact on both Israelis and Palestinians. For Israelis, it was a period marked by uncertainty and fear. The constant threat of violence and the economic hardships stemming from the Intifada took a significant toll on Israeli society. Conversely, for Palestinians, the Intifada represented a time of hope and sacrifice. It demonstrated that Palestinians were united in their quest for independence and instilled a sense of empowerment among them. It was a period that gave rise to a new generation of Palestinian activists and leaders. The First Intifada also had a notable impact on the international community. It spotlighted the plight of the Palestinian people and exerted pressure on Israel to engage in peace negotiations.

Legacy and Ongoing Struggle

The First Intifada remains a multifaceted and contentious event in the history of the Israeli-Palestinian conflict. To some, it represents a heroic struggle for freedom, while for others, it serves as a reminder of a period marked by violence and bloodshed. Regardless of one's perspective, the First Intifada was undeniably a pivotal juncture in the Israeli-Palestinian conflict. It demonstrated the Palestinians' unwavering determination to fight for their independence and compelled the Israeli government to negotiate with the PLO. The legacy of the First Intifada continues to resonate in contemporary times. It serves as an enduring source of inspiration for Palestinians in their ongoing quest for independence and remains a significant point of contention in the Israeli-Palestinian relationship.

In the chapters to come, we will delve into the continued struggles and attempts at resolution in this enduring and deeply complex conflict.

Chapter 6

The Oslo Accords

In 1993 and 1995, a pivotal moment in the Israeli-Palestinian conflict materialized through the Oslo Accords— a series of agreements brokered between Israel and the Palestine Liberation Organization (PLO) with the objective of establishing a two-state solution. The Oslo Accords constituted a groundbreaking development in the Israeli-Palestinian peace process. Notably, they marked the first official recognition between Israel and the PLO and laid the groundwork for the Palestinian Authority (PA), the governing body for Palestinians in the West Bank and Gaza Strip.

Yitzhak Rabin (right), with Yasser Arafat and Shimon Peres. (Saar Yaacov/Israel GPO)
THE OSLO ACCORDS: *A Framework for Peace*

The Oslo Accords, while complex and subject to various interpretations, were structured in two principal parts:

i. The Oslo I Accord (1993): This initial agreement granted the PA limited self-rule in the West Bank and Gaza Strip. It marked a significant departure from the status quo, in which Israel had maintained direct control over these territories. Under the Oslo I Accord, Palestinians began to exercise limited autonomy over certain aspects of governance, paving the way for the establishment of the Palestinian Authority.

i. The Oslo II Accord (1995): Building upon the progress made with the Oslo I Accord, the Oslo II Accord extended the PA's self-rule and established a timeline for final status negotiations. These negotiations were intended to conclude within five years and address critical issues such as the borders of a future Palestinian state, the status of Jerusalem, the rights of Palestinian refugees, and the nature of security arrangements between the two states.

Challenges and Controversies Surrounding the Oslo Accords
While the Oslo Accords were a noteworthy achievement, they were far from being a panacea for the Israeli-Palestinian conflict. Numerous complications and challenges accompanied their implementation, and interpretations frequently diverged between the two parties.

Implementing the Oslo Accords was a monumental task, rife with intricate challenges. It marked a pivotal shift in the Israeli-Palestinian conflict, but its execution was far from straightforward. The transfer of authority to the Palestinian Authority (PA) over civil and security matters, as outlined in the accords, was met with resistance from both sides. Palestinians sought greater autonomy, while Israelis grappled with concerns about their security. This fundamental shift in governance structures prompted a complex adjustment period. One of the central provisions of the Oslo Accords was the withdrawal of Israeli forces from certain areas of the West Bank and Gaza Strip. However, this move faced substantial resistance, particularly from Israeli settlers and right-wing factions who vehemently opposed relinquishing control over these territories. The Israeli government found itself navigating a delicate balancing act between upholding its commitments under the accords and addressing domestic opposition.

The establishment of security cooperation mechanisms between Israel and the PA was another crucial yet contentious component of the Oslo Accords. While the agreements called for joint security efforts to maintain stability, it was met with skepticism and mistrust on both sides. The legacy of decades of conflict, mistrust, and violence cast a shadow over the prospects of cooperative security measures, making the establishment of these mechanisms a challenging endeavor. Furthermore, interpretational differences between the two parties further complicated the peace process. Disagreements arose over the interpretation of key clauses and the sequence of steps outlined in the accords. Accusations of non-compliance with the terms of the agreements were exchanged, leading to frustrations and deepening mistrust. These disputes were not merely theoretical but had tangible consequences on the ground, impacting the daily lives of Israelis and Palestinians.

The issue of Israeli settlements in the West Bank and Gaza Strip, though critically important, was not explicitly addressed in the Oslo Accords. This omission proved to be a significant stumbling block in the peace process. Israel continued to expand settlements, making the prospects of a two-state solution more complex. The growth of these settlements altered the physical and demographic landscape, raising questions about the viability of a future Palestinian state. Settlement expansion remains a core point of contention and a substantial hurdle in the pursuit of peace. Controversy surrounding the Oslo Accords was not confined to one side of the conflict; it reverberated within both Israel and Palestine. While some Israelis believed that the agreements made undue concessions to the Palestinians, there were also Palestinians who felt they did not go far enough in addressing their aspirations for statehood and self-determination. This internal debate underscored the complexities and divergent opinions within each community regarding the path to peace and the perceived trade-offs involved.

The Oslo Accords, with all their intricacies and challenges, represented a landmark in the Israeli-Palestinian conflict. They marked a significant departure from the status quo, offering hope and the potential for lasting peace. However, they also underscored the immense complexities that underlie the pursuit of peace in one of the world's most protracted conflicts. As we continue to explore the multifaceted layers of this enduring narrative in the forthcoming chapters, we will encounter the enduring efforts and ongoing debates that shape the path to peace in the region.

The Impact of the Oslo Accords

The Oslo Accords held a profound influence on both Israelis and Palestinians. For Israelis, the agreements symbolized a beacon of hope and optimism. They fostered the belief that peace with the Palestinians was not only attainable but sustainable. The accords signified a fundamental shift in the status quo and offered the promise of a future where Israelis and Palestinians could live side by side in peace. Conversely, for Palestinians, the Oslo Accords presented an opportunity to actualize their long-standing aspirations for independence. They envisioned these agreements as the pathway to a Palestinian state in the West Bank and Gaza Strip, ending decades of Israeli occupation. It was a moment of genuine optimism among Palestinians who had endured the hardships of occupation and the struggle for self-determination. The Oslo Accords also resonated on the international stage. The international community welcomed the agreements and pledged its support for the peace process. World leaders saw the Oslo Accords as a significant step toward resolving one of the world's most protracted and contentious conflicts.

The Legacy of the Oslo Accords

The Oslo Accords, a momentous endeavor aimed at establishing a two-state solution in the Israeli-Palestinian conflict, ultimately fell short of achieving its lofty goal. Several factors contributed to their erosion, marking a poignant chapter in the history of this enduring conflict.

Firstly, the outbreak of the Second Intifada in 2000 shook the foundations of the Oslo Accords. This period of intensified violence, characterized by terror attacks and reprisals, rapidly eroded the trust and goodwill that had been painstakingly established through the accords. The conflict descended into a maelstrom of insecurity and fear, casting a long shadow over the prospects for peace. The violence of the Second Intifada marked a grave setback for the peace process, as the human toll and bitterness on both sides created an atmosphere of deep distrust. The continuous expansion of Israeli settlements in the West Bank, in defiance of the Oslo Accords' provisions, added another layer of complexity to the quest for a two-state solution. Settlement expansion altered the physical and demographic landscape of the occupied territories, making the establishment of a viable Palestinian state increasingly challenging. It significantly impacted the territorial contiguity required for a future Palestinian state, raising questions about its feasibility. The settlements issue remains one of the most contentious and daunting obstacles in the pursuit of peace.

Additionally, the failure of both sides to reach a final agreement on core issues such as borders, the status of Jerusalem, the rights of Palestinian refugees, and security arrangements hindered the Oslo Accords' progress. While the accords set a timeline for concluding final status negotiations within five years, these talks failed to produce a mutually acceptable agreement. The inability to bridge the deep divides on these fundamental issues left the peace process in a state of stagnation. The quest for a resolution that could address the deeply rooted concerns and aspirations of both Israelis and Palestinians appeared increasingly elusive.

Despite these formidable challenges, the Oslo Accords remain a significant chapter in the history of the Israeli-Palestinian conflict. They exemplified the potential for both sides to engage in negotiations for a peaceful resolution to the conflict. These agreements were a testament to the power of diplomacy and dialogue, offering a glimmer of hope that the deeply entrenched and contentious conflict could be resolved through compromise and cooperation. Though they ultimately fell short of their objectives, the Oslo Accords remain an enduring symbol of the ongoing quest for peace in a region marked by complex historical and geopolitical factors. As we continue to explore the intricate and evolving narrative of the Israeli-Palestinian conflict in the chapters ahead, we will encounter the ongoing efforts, challenges, and aspirations that shape the path to peace in the region.

Legacy and Ongoing Debate

The legacy of the Oslo Accords is a topic of ongoing debate, reflecting the multifaceted nature of this pivotal moment in the Israeli-Palestinian conflict. The differing perspectives on the Oslo Accords have profound implications for the future of the peace process and the ultimate resolution of this enduring conflict.

Some view the Oslo Accords as a regrettable misstep, pointing to their failure to deliver a lasting peace. This perspective argues that the Oslo process allowed for the entrenchment of the Israeli occupation and the expansion of settlements in the West Bank, ultimately making the prospects for a two-state solution more daunting. Critics contend that the Oslo Accords, while well-intentioned, did not do enough to address core issues such as the settlements, borders, and the status of Jerusalem. As a result, the conflict continued to fester, leading to increased frustration and skepticism about the viability of a two-state solution. Conversely, others see the Oslo Accords as an essential step in the peace process. They believe that the agreements, despite their imperfections, paved the way for critical diplomatic and institutional developments. The establishment of the Palestinian Authority (PA) in the West Bank and Gaza Strip, as a result of the Oslo Accords, created a framework for Palestinian self-governance. These proponents argue that the Oslo Accords laid the foundation for the development of conditions necessary for a future Palestinian state. While not a final solution, the accords represented a significant departure from the status quo, offering a potential path towards self-determination for the Palestinian people.

Regardless of one's perspective, it is undeniable that the Oslo Accords constituted a seminal moment in the Israeli-Palestinian conflict. These agreements shaped discussions regarding the future of both Israelis and Palestinians, laying bare the intricate challenges and opportunities embedded in the pursuit of peace.

As we continue to explore the multifaceted layers of this enduring narrative in the forthcoming chapters, we will delve into the ongoing efforts, challenges, and aspirations that shape the path to peace in the region. From the hopeful beginnings of the Oslo Accords to the subsequent challenges and disappointments, the story of this conflict remains a poignant and vital exploration of human history and the enduring quest for peace in a troubled land. The Oslo Accords, with all their complexities and controversies, serve as a reminder of the relentless pursuit of peace in the face of entrenched historical and geopolitical complexities.

Chapter 7

The Second Intifada

The Second Intifada, often referred to as the al-Aqsa Intifada, represented a harrowing and deeply tumultuous period in the Israeli-Palestinian conflict. Spanning over five years, from its outbreak in September 2000, it was marked by sustained violence and suffering on both sides. The catalyst for this tumultuous chapter was the visit of Israeli opposition leader Ariel Sharon to the Temple Mount, a site of profound religious significance for both Jews and Muslims. Sharon's visit, seen as a provocation by many Palestinians, ignited widespread protests and outbreaks of violence. The situation rapidly escalated, leading to a protracted and violent confrontation.

An Israeli Border Policeman and a Palestinian scream at each other face-to-face in the Old City of Jerusalem, Oct. 13, 2000. - REUTERS/Amit Shabi

THE SECOND INTIFADA was characterized by a range of violent acts, including suicide bombings, shootings, and attacks on Israeli civilians. These acts of violence created a pervasive atmosphere of insecurity and fear, affecting the daily lives of both Israelis and Palestinians. The Palestinian territories, particularly the Gaza Strip and the West Bank, bore the brunt of this violence, with a significant loss of life and physical devastation. In response to the violence, the Israeli military launched a crackdown on Palestinians. This crackdown involved targeted killings, mass arrests, and the implementation of strict security measures. The confrontations between Israeli forces and Palestinian militants were both frequent and fierce, leading to further casualties and suffering. The consequences of the Second Intifada were devastating for both Israelis and Palestinians. Over 4,000 Palestinians and more than 1,000 Israelis lost their lives during this period. The human toll of the conflict was compounded by severe economic repercussions. The violence disrupted daily life, strained the economies of both Israel and the Palestinian territories, and deepened the socio-economic challenges faced by both communities.

The Second Intifada finally came to an end in 2005 with the signing of the Sharm el-Sheikh Agreement. This agreement called for a ceasefire and a return to peace negotiations, marking a temporary respite from the relentless violence. However, despite these diplomatic efforts, the subsequent peace talks yielded no concrete results, leaving the Israeli-Palestinian conflict unresolved. The deep-rooted issues that fueled the Second Intifada, including the status of Jerusalem, borders, refugees, and security, remained unresolved, perpetuating the cycle of violence and distrust in the region.

The Impact of the Second Intifada

The Second Intifada, also known as the al-Aqsa Intifada, left an indelible mark on the Israeli-Palestinian conflict and had profound implications for the people on both sides. For Israelis, the Second Intifada was a time fraught with fear and uncertainty. The constant threat of violence, including suicide bombings and attacks on civilians, had a profound impact on Israeli society. Daily life was marked by heightened security measures, and the economic hardships brought about by the intifada took a toll on many. Fear and a pervasive sense of insecurity became part of the Israeli experience during this tumultuous period. Conversely, for Palestinians, the Second Intifada represented a time of hope and sacrifice. It served as a testament to their unwavering commitment to their quest for independence and self-determination. The intifada was seen as a collective effort to resist the occupation and assert their right to a sovereign state. It bolstered a sense of empowerment among Palestinians and a belief in their ability to affect change.

On the international stage, the Second Intifada spotlighted the plight of the Palestinian people and the broader Israeli-Palestinian conflict. It garnered international attention and exerted significant pressure on Israel to engage in peace negotiations. The global community, witnessing the suffering and violence, called for a resolution to the conflict and expressed support for the Palestinian cause. The legacy of the Second Intifada is multifaceted and contentious. To some, it represents a heroic struggle for freedom and independence, a testament to the resilience of the Palestinian people. Others, however, remember it for the violence and bloodshed it unleashed, with deep scars that still linger.

Regardless of one's perspective, it is undeniable that the Second Intifada constituted a significant turning point in the Israeli-Palestinian conflict. It demonstrated the Palestinians' continued determination to fight for their independence, adding complexity to the pursuit of a two-state solution. The legacy of the Second Intifada continues to influence contemporary events, serving as an enduring source of inspiration for Palestinians in their ongoing struggle for independence. It also remains a point of tension and contention between Israelis and

Palestinians, a reminder of the challenges and aspirations embedded within this enduring narrative.

THE FUTURE OF THE ISRAELI-Palestinian Conflict

The path forward for the Israeli-Palestinian conflict remains shrouded in uncertainty, with deep-seated divisions, persistent violence, and unresolved issues casting a long shadow over the prospects for peace.

However, history has shown that peace is attainable even in the most protracted and seemingly intractable conflicts. The Israeli-Palestinian conflict is no exception to this potential. There have been numerous instances in which seemingly irreconcilable adversaries have come to the negotiating table and, against all odds, found common ground for peace. The responsibility for this monumental task lies with the leaders of Israel and Palestine. If they choose the path of peace, it will demand the courage to make concessions, the wisdom to navigate complex issues, and the vision to build a future of coexistence. This challenging journey, though daunting, remains a real and achievable possibility. As the dialogue for peace persists, the hope for a peaceful resolution to this enduring conflict remains alive. It is a testament to the enduring human spirit, the power of diplomacy, and the potential for reconciliation and coexistence. The road ahead may be fraught with challenges, but it is also illuminated by the possibility of a brighter, more peaceful future for all those affected by the Israeli-Palestinian conflict.

Chapter 8

The 2006 Lebanon War

The 2006 Lebanon War, often referred to as the July War, stands as a somber and pivotal chapter in the ongoing Israeli-Palestinian conflict. Lasting for 34 intense and destructive days, this military conflict pitted Israel against Hezbollah, a Lebanese militant group, and cast a long shadow over the region. The war ignited on July 12, 2006, when Hezbollah launched a cross-border raid, capturing two Israeli soldiers and tragically killing three others. In response to this provocative act, Israel swiftly retaliated with a massive airstrike campaign on Lebanon. What began as a localized conflict quickly escalated into a full-scale war with far-reaching implications.

The 2006 Lebanon War underscored several significant dynamics in the broader context of the Israeli-Palestinian conflict. Firstly, it highlighted the growing power and influence of Hezbollah in the region. As a non-state actor, Hezbollah's ability to hold its ground and engage in prolonged conflict with one of the most formidable military forces in the Middle East sent a strong message about the changing landscape of power and influence in the region. Secondly, the war made it abundantly clear that Israel was prepared to employ military force as a means to achieve its objectives. It demonstrated that Israel was willing to engage in large-scale military operations to protect its interests and security. However, the consequences of the 2006 Lebanon War extended beyond the immediate military clashes. The war had a devastating impact on Lebanon, resulting in profound loss and destruction. Over 1,000 Lebanese civilians lost their lives, and hundreds of thousands were displaced from their homes. The economic toll was also staggering, with billions of dollars in damage inflicted on Lebanon's infrastructure and economy.

The 2006 Lebanon War finally came to a close on August 14, 2006, with a ceasefire brokered by the United Nations. While the ceasefire brought an end to the active fighting, it did not address the fundamental and underlying issues in the Israeli-Palestinian conflict. The ceasefire represented a temporary respite from the violence, but it did not offer a comprehensive solution to the complex challenges and disputes that continue to define the region. The 2006 Lebanon War serves as a stark reminder of the persistent instability and uncertainty in the Middle East. It underscores the profound impact of regional actors like Hezbollah and the role of military force in shaping the Israeli-Palestinian conflict. As we move forward through the following chapters, we will continue to explore the intricate and interconnected dimensions of this enduring narrative.

THE IMPACT OF THE 2006 Lebanon War

The 2006 Lebanon War, with its profound implications, left a lasting impact on various stakeholders and continues to influence the dynamics of the Israeli-Palestinian conflict.

For Israelis, the war served as a stark reminder of the threats posed by Hezbollah and other militant groups in the region. It underscored the persistent challenges to Israeli security and led to increased public support for the Israeli government's hard-line policies, driven by the perception of a need to safeguard the nation against such threats. Conversely, for the Lebanese, the 2006 Lebanon War was a time of immense suffering. The conflict caused widespread death and destruction, displacing hundreds of thousands of people and leaving deep scars on the nation. The economic repercussions of the war were also profound, affecting livelihoods and the overall stability of the Lebanese economy. The war also had a significant impact on the international community. It drew global attention to the dangers posed by militant groups like Hezbollah in the region, raising concerns about regional instability and security. The conflict exerted pressure on Israel to engage in peace negotiations with the Palestinians, as it highlighted the need for diplomatic solutions to the long-standing issues in the Middle East.

The legacy of the 2006 Lebanon War is complex and remains a subject of contention. It is remembered by some as a necessary response to Hezbollah's attack, while others view it as a war that could have been avoided. This difference in perspective underscores the complexity of the conflict and the challenges associated with its resolution. Regardless of one's viewpoint, the 2006 Lebanon War is an undeniable turning point in the Israeli-Palestinian conflict. It demonstrated the power and influence of Hezbollah in the region and made clear that Israel was willing to employ military force to achieve its strategic objectives. The legacy of the 2006 Lebanon War continues to reverberate in the region, contributing to ongoing tensions and serving as a reminder of the complex and interconnected issues that shape the Israeli-Palestinian conflict.

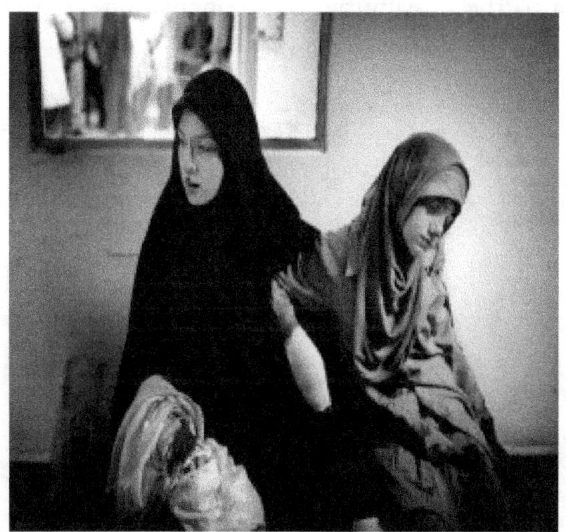

Aftermath of the 'July War' (https://marcodilauro.com/features/lebanon-july-war)

THE FUTURE OF THE ISRAELI-Palestinian Conflict

The future of the Israeli-Palestinian conflict remains shrouded in uncertainty, with deep-seated divisions, ongoing violence, and unresolved issues that challenge the prospects for a peaceful resolution.

However, it's crucial to recognize that peace remains attainable. History is replete with examples of conflicts that have found peaceful resolutions, and the Israeli-Palestinian conflict is no exception to this potential. The quest for peace is an enduring aspiration, and there is room for hope in the pursuit of a just and lasting resolution.

Ultimately, the responsibility for peace lies in the hands of the leaders of Israel and Palestine. Their decisions will shape the course of this conflict, and if they choose the path of peace, it will require the courage to make compromises, the wisdom to navigate complex issues, and the vision to create a future marked by coexistence and prosperity. The road to peace may be challenging, and it may demand difficult choices and significant efforts. However, it is a path that holds the promise of a brighter and more peaceful future for all those affected by the Israeli-Palestinian conflict. While the future may seem uncertain, it remains open to the possibilities of reconciliation, cooperation, and a just resolution to this enduring conflict.

Chapter 9

The 2014 Gaza War

The 2014 Gaza War, also known as Operation Protective Edge, represents a pivotal and tragic episode in the ongoing Israeli-Palestinian conflict. This military confrontation unfolded between Israel and the Palestinian militant group Hamas and has left a lasting impact on the region. The conflict erupted on July 8, 2014, and extended over a grueling 50-day period, making it the deadliest and most protracted engagement between the two parties since the 2008–2009 Gaza War.

The origins of the 2014 Gaza War can be traced to a series of Israeli airstrikes on Gaza, which were initiated in response to ongoing rocket attacks launched by Hamas militants. Simultaneously, the Israeli military launched a ground invasion of Gaza, leading to a significant escalation of hostilities. In retaliation, Hamas fired thousands of rockets into Israel, further intensifying the conflict. The consequences of the 2014 Gaza War were devastating, particularly for the Gaza Strip. Over 2,200 Palestinians lost their lives, a tragic toll that included more than 500 children. Additionally, more than 10,000 Palestinians were injured, and hundreds of thousands were forced to flee their homes due to the destruction and violence. The economic impact on Gaza was profound, with billions of dollars in damage inflicted on the local economy, causing long-lasting hardship for the population.

Israel also faced significant losses during the conflict, with over 70 casualties, including six civilians, and more than 500 Israelis injured. The economic implications of the war were felt as well, as the Israeli economy grappled with the aftermath of the protracted conflict. The fighting finally came to a halt on August 26, 2014, when a ceasefire was brokered by Egypt. While the ceasefire ended the immediate violence, it did not resolve the deep-seated issues and disputes at the core of the Israeli-Palestinian conflict. The 2014 Gaza War underscores the continued complexity and volatility of the Israeli-Palestinian conflict. It stands as a stark reminder of the human toll and economic devastation that such conflicts bring, and it serves as a testament to the urgent need for a comprehensive and lasting resolution to the ongoing tensions in the region. As we move forward through the following chapters, we will delve deeper into the intricate and interconnected dimensions of this enduring narrative.

The Impact of the 2014 Gaza War

The repercussions of the 2014 Gaza War resonated deeply, leaving a lasting impact on both Israelis and Palestinians, as well as garnering international attention.

For Israelis, the conflict served as a stark and unsettling reminder of the ongoing threats posed by Hamas and other militant groups operating in the region. The indiscriminate rocket attacks and the scale of violence during the war heightened security concerns, contributing to increased public support for the Israeli government's hard-line policies, especially in regard to national security. On the Palestinian side, the 2014 Gaza War brought immense suffering. It left in its wake widespread death and destruction, causing deep trauma and despair among the Gazan population. The conflict forced hundreds of thousands of Palestinians to flee their homes, often with only the possessions they could carry, creating a humanitarian crisis. Moreover, the war had a catastrophic impact on the Gazan economy, further compounding the daily hardships faced by the local population.

At least 18,000 homes in Gaza were destroyed during Israel's 50-day military operation
(https://www.bbc.com/news/world-middle-east-39118231)

THE INTERNATIONAL COMMUNITY'S attention was drawn to the 2014 Gaza War due to the scale of the violence and the humanitarian crisis it engendered. The conflict underscored the complex security challenges posed by militant groups in the region, with particular emphasis on Hamas, and brought the Israeli-Palestinian conflict back into the global spotlight. The war also intensified pressure on Israel to engage in meaningful peace negotiations with the Palestinians, reflecting the international community's concern for a resolution to this protracted conflict. As we progress through the subsequent chapters, we will continue to delve deeper into the multifaceted dimensions of the Israeli-Palestinian conflict, striving to understand the complexities, challenges, and potential pathways toward peace in this enduring narrative.

The Legacy of the 2014 Gaza War

The legacy of the 2014 Gaza War is marked by complexity and controversy, as different perspectives shape the understanding of this pivotal chapter in the Israeli-Palestinian conflict. For some, the war is seen as a necessary and justified response to the relentless rocket attacks by Hamas, emphasizing the imperative to protect Israeli civilians from indiscriminate threats. In this view, the conflict becomes a stark illustration of Israel's commitment to safeguarding its population.

Conversely, others argue that the war could have been avoided through diplomatic means, potentially sparing the immense suffering and destruction experienced by Gazans. This perspective highlights the necessity of pursuing peaceful negotiations over military action. Regardless of one's stance, the 2014 Gaza War undeniably signifies a significant turning point in the Israeli-Palestinian conflict. It underscored the formidable influence and resilience of Hamas in the region and reiterated Israel's willingness to employ military force to secure its objectives. The legacy of the 2014 Gaza War endures, casting a long shadow over the relationship between Israel and Gaza, and it continues to pose challenges to regional stability. The intricacies surrounding this chapter remain relevant to contemporary events in the Israeli-Palestinian conflict, emphasizing the importance of finding a sustainable and peaceful resolution to these enduring tensions. As we navigate through the forthcoming chapters, we will delve deeper into the complexities, challenges, and potential pathways towards peace in this ongoing narrative.

Chapter 10

The Current Situation

The Israeli-Palestinian conflict, spanning over seven decades, stands as one of the world's most enduring and intricate disputes, leaving a profound impact on the Middle East and beyond. Rooted in historical grievances and territorial disputes, it continues to cast a long shadow, generating ongoing tension and human suffering.

AS WE ASSESS THE CURRENT state of affairs, the grim reality is that peace remains as elusive as ever. In the absence of a comprehensive peace agreement, the region is marred by continuing violence and unresolved differences on core issues. The prospect of a two-state solution, which envisions an independent Palestinian state living alongside Israel, faces a significant hurdle – Israel's continued expansion of settlements in the occupied West Bank. These settlements not only present a significant barrier to achieving peace but also erode the territorial contiguity of a future Palestinian state. The Palestinian Authority (PA), entrusted with the governance of the West Bank and Gaza Strip, faces formidable challenges in navigating the complex landscape. Internal divisions within the Palestinian leadership have led to political fragmentation, making it difficult to present a united front in negotiations with Israel. The PA also grapples with the Herculean task of providing essential services and improving the living conditions of the Palestinian population under the constraints of occupation. This includes addressing economic hardship, high unemployment rates, and restricted access to resources – factors that intensify the suffering of Palestinians.

In Gaza, a distinct and tumultuous territory, the situation is even direr. It remains under the control of Hamas, an organization designated as a terrorist group by several countries, including the United States and the European Union. The consequences of this designation and the ongoing conflict have been devastating. A recurring cycle of violence characterizes the region, with Hamas firing rockets into Israel and Israel responding with airstrikes. This repetitive pattern inflicts substantial damage, resulting in the loss of innocent lives and widespread destruction in Gaza. The territory's population has borne the brunt of this ongoing crisis. The international community, acutely aware of the ramifications of the Israeli-Palestinian conflict, has not remained passive. Over the years, it has passed numerous United Nations resolutions that advocate for a two-state solution, recognizing the imperative of a Palestinian state living side by side with Israel in peace and security. These resolutions underscore the international community's commitment to a just and lasting resolution of the conflict. Regrettably, while they express the will of the global community, they have not yielded effective implementation, leaving the conflict unresolved.

The United States, traditionally a key mediator in the peace process, has faced shifting priorities and complex challenges in recent years. In 2017, the Trump administration marked a significant departure from past U.S. policy by disengaging from the peace process. This disengagement was coupled with a controversial move of the U.S. Embassy from Tel Aviv to Jerusalem. The recognition of Jerusalem as Israel's capital was met with widespread international condemnation, and its ramifications continue to influence the peace process. In contrast, the Biden administration has signalled a renewed interest in addressing the Israeli-Palestinian conflict. However, the specifics of its approach and the extent of its involvement remain uncertain. These uncertainties raise questions about the future trajectory of U.S. engagement in this enduring conflict, leaving stakeholders cautiously optimistic.

The humanitarian situation in the Palestinian territories remains a subject of deep concern. In the West Bank and Gaza Strip, the population continues to grapple with economic hardship, high unemployment rates, and limited access to resources. These challenges are exacerbated by the constraints of the Israeli occupation, which restrict economic development and limit the Palestinians' ability to exercise self-determination. Jerusalem, a city claimed as a capital by both Israelis and Palestinians, stands at the center of a highly contentious dispute. Israel asserts sovereignty over the entire city, a claim recognized by a handful of countries. In contrast, the majority of the international community regards Jerusalem's status as a final status issue, subject to negotiation. The city's profound religious, historical, and political significance further complicates efforts to resolve this central issue.

Security concerns continue to play a dominant role in shaping the dynamics of the conflict. Israel emphasizes its right to self-defense against security threats, particularly the indiscriminate rocket attacks launched from Gaza by militant groups, including Hamas. The Palestinian leadership and many in the international community contend that the Israeli occupation and its accompanying policies constitute the core issue, perpetuating a cycle of violence and instability in the region. In recent years, sporadic episodes of violence and conflict have erupted, leading to casualties on both sides and further exacerbating tensions. These incidents underscore the volatility of the situation and the ever-present risk of escalation, contributing to an environment where mistrust and uncertainty prevail. The issue of Palestinian refugees, stemming from the 1948 war, remains a significant and highly sensitive challenge. Many Palestinians and their descendants are registered as refugees, and the right of return continues to be a deeply held aspiration and point of contention. Resolution of this issue remains a central concern in any comprehensive peace agreement.

The future of the Israeli-Palestinian conflict remains uncertain, with both sides deeply divided on key issues. The quest for a two-state solution, a vision of an independent Palestinian state coexisting with Israel, faces formidable obstacles. Settlement expansion, political fragmentation among the Palestinians, and ongoing security concerns continue to complicate the path to peace. Nevertheless, it is vital to remember that peace is attainable. History offers numerous examples of conflicts that have found peaceful resolutions, and the Israeli-Palestinian conflict is no exception. The ultimate decision rests with the leaders of Israel and Palestine. Should they choose the path of peace, it will necessitate courage, vision, and a willingness to make difficult concessions. The international community also plays a pivotal role in the pursuit of peace. By applying diplomatic pressure on both Israel and Palestine to engage constructively in negotiations, providing critical financial and technical support to the Palestinian people, and affirming its commitment to a two-state solution, the global community can contribute to the peace process.

The Israeli-Palestinian conflict is undeniably complex and formidable, but it is not insurmountable. The possibility of peace endures, waiting to be realized through determination and compromise. In the chapters that follow, we will delve deeper into the multifaceted dimensions of this enduring conflict, striving to comprehend the complexities, challenges, and potential pathways toward a just and lasting peace. The narrative of the Israeli-Palestinian conflict is one of human suffering and aspiration, and it remains an urgent and vital issue in today's world.

Chapter 11

The Path to Peace

The Israeli-Palestinian conflict, a protracted and intricate struggle that has afflicted generations of Israelis and Palestinians, continues to be a source of suffering and instability in the region. While it may seem that a peaceful resolution is elusive, the desire for peace persists on both sides. Over the years, numerous attempts at peace negotiations have been made, underscoring that the path to peace remains a viable option. To embark on this path to peace, several crucial steps must be taken, each demanding unwavering commitment and effort from all parties involved.

In the pursuit of peace in the Israeli-Palestinian conflict, there are critical steps that must be undertaken. The persistent cycle of violence between Israel and Palestine, a constant obstacle to meaningful peace negotiations, necessitates an immediate and sustained cessation of hostilities. Violence, marked by destructive actions and deep-seated mistrust, only serves to perpetuate a vicious circle of animosity. The first and most vital stride toward peace involves both sides recognizing that violence is not a path to resolution, and that only peaceful negotiations offer hope for a lasting accord. In parallel, building trust stands as a fundamental building block of any successful peace process. This complex and challenging endeavor is pivotal to paving the way for the necessary compromises for a peaceful resolution. Trust is born from a mutual confidence in each other's unwavering commitment to peace, offering a foundation upon which meaningful negotiations can occur.

The pursuit of a two-state solution, an arrangement envisioning an independent Palestinian state coexisting alongside the State of Israel, is widely accepted as the most pragmatic framework for achieving a peaceful resolution to the conflict. This vision, supported by both Israelis and Palestinians in the past, underscores the potential for compromise and coexistence. Negotiating and reaching a comprehensive two-state solution is paramount to ending the ongoing conflict. However, the path to peace is strewn with obstacles that require deliberate resolution. Key issues that must be addressed include the delineation of borders for each state, the status of Jerusalem, and the right of return for Palestinian refugees. These issues, profoundly complex and emotionally charged, have remained at the core of the conflict for decades. Finding resolutions necessitates courage, flexibility, and a willingness to make difficult concessions from both sides.

Clarifying the borders of Israel and a prospective Palestinian state is fundamental, ensuring territorial integrity for both parties. The issue of Jerusalem, a city claimed as a capital by both Israelis and Palestinians, remains central. Resolution may involve shared sovereignty, international administration, or another innovative solution respecting the city's deep historical and religious significance. Addressing the right of return for Palestinian refugees, another pivotal issue, touches on the aspirations of individuals and the collective wishes of Palestinians displaced since the 1948 war. A fair and equitable resolution that respects the rights and dignity of all parties involved is essential. Furthermore, achieving a peace agreement, a significant milestone in the peace process, must be rigorously implemented. This process demands unwavering commitment and cooperation from both Israelis and Palestinians. International support and monitoring are essential to ensure that all parties adhere to the terms of the agreement. International stakeholders play a pivotal role in overseeing and ensuring the faithful implementation of any peace accord, safeguarding its integrity and sustainability.

The international community can contribute to the peace process in several meaningful ways:

Diplomatic Pressure: Exerting diplomatic pressure on both Israel and Palestine is a crucial tool in the international community's arsenal for encouraging constructive negotiations. Such pressure is imperative in breaking the ongoing cycle of violence and stagnation, urging the involved parties to return to the negotiating table. This diplomatic intervention may also encompass the counsel to refrain from actions that hinder peace efforts, such as unilateral moves or escalatory measures. Encouraging a renewed commitment to the principles of a two-state solution, where an independent Palestinian state coexists alongside Israel, is a central component of this diplomatic endeavor. The collective voice of the international community can serve as a catalyst for renewed dialogue, bridging the divides and reminding all stakeholders of the global significance of a peaceful resolution to the Israeli-Palestinian conflict.

Financial and Technical Support: The international community can provide financial and technical support to address the profound economic and humanitarian challenges faced by the Palestinian population. Such support plays a pivotal role in improving living conditions and fostering an environment that is more conducive to negotiations. Investments in economic development, infrastructure, education, and healthcare are not only essential for the well-being of Palestinians but also demonstrate a commitment to their future and a recognition of their rights. The alleviation of economic hardships and improvement of living standards can significantly contribute to creating a conducive atmosphere for constructive negotiations. Moreover, the international community can offer technical assistance in building essential governance structures and institutions that are vital for statehood, thereby reinforcing the capacity of Palestinians to govern themselves effectively.

Peace Monitoring: To ensure the faithful and effective implementation of any peace agreement, international stakeholders can participate in a process of monitoring compliance. This monitoring, conducted with the consent and cooperation of all parties involved, provides transparency, accountability, and the necessary confidence required to maintain the integrity of the peace process. It serves as a safeguard against potential violations and disputes, thereby building trust among the parties involved. By providing an external oversight mechanism, peace monitoring can contribute to the prevention of disputes and the resolution of those that do arise. Moreover, it helps maintain the adherence to the terms of the agreement, ensuring that both Israelis and Palestinians remain committed to the path of peaceful coexistence.

The Israeli-Palestinian conflict is undoubtedly complex and formidable, but it is not insurmountable. The desire for peace is shared by many on both sides, and history teaches us that even the most protracted and entrenched conflicts can find peaceful resolutions. The key to success lies in the resolve and willingness to compromise. A just and lasting peace is attainable, provided that all parties involved, together with the international community, remain committed to the pursuit of dialogue, understanding, and cooperation. Both Israelis and Palestinians have the potential to work together to transform their shared future, putting an end to the suffering and instability that have afflicted the region for generations.